HANS ZIMMER

BIOGRAPHY

The Genius who Redefined Film music

By

WILLIAM C. WATT

TABLE OF CONTENT

CONCLUSION

INTRODUCTION

When it comes to artists like Hans Zimmer, it's impossible to underestimate the seismic impact one person can have on the worlds of music and movies. Zimmer, a maestro who has spent decades creating unique soundscapes, has changed the fundamental essence of film composing, permanently altering how viewers experience cinema. From the thrilling suspense of Inception to the majestic triumph of The Lion King, his music crosses genres, bridging the gap between symphonic grandeur and electronic innovation. Beyond the awards and renowned songs, Zimmer's narrative exemplifies endless inventiveness, unwavering enthusiasm, and an unwavering ambition to push the limits of what music can do.

Hans Zimmer, who was born in Germany and later moved to Hollywood, created emotional experiences rather than just music. His soundtracks have become cultural icons, echoing in the minds of millions and influencing countless blockbuster films. Zimmer's influence stretches far beyond movie theatres, having won numerous Academy Awards, Golden Globes, and Grammys. He moulded an era's sound, making an enduring influence not only on cinema soundtracks but also on the whole music industry.

What makes Zimmer's journey even more remarkable is his ability to adapt, invent, and evolve with each endeavour. Whether collaborating with creative directors such as Christopher Nolan and Ridley Scott, or guiding the next generation of composers, he has never been satisfied with his accomplishments. Instead, he continues to push himself, exploring new sound worlds that combine conventional orchestration with cutting-edge electronics to create something all his own.

As you explore Hans Zimmer's biography, you'll discover the narrative of a man who turned problems into opportunities, revolutionised film music, and influenced many musicians around the world. This is more than a biography; it's the story of a visionary who altered how we listen, feel, and perceive the world around us.

CHAPTER 1

WHO IS HANS ZIMMER?

Hans Zimmer is a renowned German composer and music producer whose work has significantly altered the landscape of cinema scoring. With a career spanning four decades, Zimmer has composed some of cinema's most unforgettable soundtracks, combining symphonic grandeur with cutting-edge electronic elements. His renowned compositions for films like *The Lion King*, *Gladiator*, *Inception*, *The Dark Knight Trilogy*, and *Interstellar* have earned him numerous accolades, including Academy Awards, Golden Globes, and Grammys. Zimmer's creative technique has revolutionised the emotional depth and storytelling potential of film music, establishing him as a trailblazer who continues to inspire and shape the sound of modern cinema.

Early life and influences (1957– 1970s)

Hans Zimmer, born on September 12, 1957, in Frankfurt, West Germany, grew up in a world that was slowly reconstructing itself after World War II. This moment of transformation and renewal in Germany had a tremendous impact on Zimmer's boyhood. He was reared in a creative household by parents who emphasised the significance of education, culture, and the arts. His mother, a great pianist, exposed him to classical music at a young age, while his father, an engineer and inventor, fostered curiosity and a propensity to experiment. This combination of artistic and intellectual influence provided fertile ground for Zimmer's growing interest in music.

Zimmer's love of music became apparent as a young boy, and his parents encouraged him to pursue it by arranging piano lessons. However, the traditional technique of learning music did not appeal to him. Zimmer was restless and considered traditional piano training too rigorous. Instead, he was drawn to the more intuitive, emotional components of music composition, preferring to experiment with melodies on his own terms. Even at such a young age, Zimmer exhibited an independent streak, predicting the inventive spirit that would eventually define his career. He famously described being expelled from eight different schools as a child, implying his rebellious attitude and refusal to adapt to normal frameworks - a trait that would eventually become his greatest strength in music.

One of the most transforming experiences for Zimmer throughout his formative years was the early death of his father when he was just six. This experience had a great influence on him, driving him to seek consolation and expression via music. In interviews, Zimmer frequently refers to music as his "best friend" during those trying times, and it was through this profound connection that he began to build his own emotional relationship with sound. The piano became more than just an instrument; it was a conduit through which he could express his sentiments of grief, wonder, and curiosity.

Growing up in a culturally diverse milieu, Zimmer was exposed to a wide range of musical influences that went beyond classical pieces. The late 1960s and early 1970s were an exciting period in music, with rock 'n' roll and experimental genres gaining prominence. The Beatles, Jimi Hendrix, and Pink Floyd were at the height of their popularity, and Zimmer was drawn to rock music's electric energy and limitless invention. This was a watershed moment in his musical career, as he began to investigate how diverse sounds and genres could be combined to create something completely new. He trained himself to play the guitar and experimented with synthesisers, an unusual instrument at the time, sparking a lifetime interest in electronic music.

Ennio Morricone, the iconic Italian composer well known for his work on spaghetti westerns, was a major early inspiration for Zimmer. The way Morricone combined traditional orchestral parts with strange sounds and instruments struck a chord with Zimmer, who regarded Morricone's work as a mirror of his desire to break free from traditional musical structures. This influence is evident in Zimmer's later works, where he frequently combines orchestral arrangements with electronic sounds to produce something both familiar and innovative.

Zimmer's love of music became stronger during his adolescence, and he began to pursue it more seriously. He joined a local band and experimented with many styles and genres, immersing himself in the emerging rock culture of the time. This time of experimentation was critical for Zimmer since it allowed him to build his sound and realise the infinite possibilities of music. During this period, he discovered the synthesiser, which eventually became a vital part of his unique style. The synthesiser enabled Zimmer to combine his love of classical music with modern rock elements, creating a world of sound possibilities that defied conventional limitations.

Zimmer's early years were also characterised by an interest in technology and how it could be used to generate new sounds. This fascination prompted him to go deeper into the realm of synthesisers, and he quickly learned how to use them to create unique pieces. The combination of technology and music became a trademark of Zimmer's work, allowing him to create compositions that were both melodically rich and texturally complex.

In the late 1970s, Zimmer made the decision to relocate to London, which proved to be a watershed moment in his life. London's lively music culture provided him with new perspectives and several opportunities to hone his skills. He started working as a session musician, collaborating with different artists and getting practical experience in recording facilities. During this period, he joined the band The

Buggles, a new wave group best known for their smash single "Video Killed the Radio Star." Zimmer performed the keyboard on this landmark track, which became the first music video to air on MTV in 1981. This experience introduced him to the realm of music production and studio recording, where he honed his talents in synthesiser programming and arrangement.

Despite the popularity of The Buggles, Zimmer recognized his true calling was elsewhere. He was more interested in how music could help storytelling, which led him to pursue a career in film score. His early exposure to a wide range of musical genres, from classical works to rock and electronic influences, gave him a diverse pallet of sounds to work with. This diversified background would eventually serve as the foundation for his own style, allowing him to compose soundtracks that were both emotionally captivating and sonically diverse.

Throughout his early years, Zimmer was inspired by the works of famous composers such as Johann Sebastian Bach and Richard Wagner, whose large orchestral pieces taught him the value of melody and harmony. However, he never lost interest in contemporary music, and he continued to study the works of artists such as Brian Eno and Kraftwerk, who pioneered the use of electronic instruments in modern composition. This combination of old and modern, traditional and experimental, became the essence of Zimmer's approach to music, which later distinguished him in the film industry.

By the end of the 1970s, Hans Zimmer had amassed a formidable skill set that blended classical background, rock influences, and a thorough understanding of electronic music. He was ready to take the next step in his career, entering the realm of film score. His childhood in Germany, his family's support, his father's terrible death, and the various musical influences he met all helped to shape his artistic personality. This identity, based on a complex tapestry of experiences and inspirations, would eventually lead him to become one of the most prominent cinema composers of his generation.

Zimmer's early life exemplifies the premise that creativity often comes from the intersection of disparate events, and his rise from a young boy in postwar Germany to a pioneering composer is nothing short of miraculous. His narrative is about more than simply skill; it's about a never-ending love of music, an insatiable curiosity, and a fearless willingness to explore the unknown. As he embarked on the next chapter of his life, Zimmer took with him the lessons, influences, and ambitions that would eventually shape him into the musical genius the world would come to know and admire.

CHAPTER 2

THE PATH TO FILM SCORING (1980s)

The 1980s was a watershed moment in Hans Zimmer's career, as he transitioned from pop music to cinema composing, where he would eventually make a lasting impression. While Zimmer's narrative is filled with incredible skill, it is also a voyage of discovery, perseverance, and reinvention. It starts with his early musical endeavours, most famously with the synth-pop band The Buggles, and ends with his breakthrough into cinema scoring with My Beautiful Laundrette and A World Apart—two productions that paved the way for his future success.

In the late 1970s, Zimmer relocated to London and immersed himself in the city's thriving music scene. He rapidly got employment as a session musician, and his skill with synthesisers made him a popular collaborator. Zimmer soon joined The Buggles, a band formed by Trevor Horn and Geoff Downes. The Buggles rose to prominence with their breakthrough single "Video Killed the Radio Star," which was published in 1979 and became the first music video to air on MTV in 1981. As The Buggles' keyboardist, Zimmer was at the vanguard of the synth-pop trend, helping to create a sound that combined electronic music with popular pop tunes.

While his time with The Buggles was brief, it provided Zimmer with vital insight into the realm of music production and introduced him to the boundless potential of synthesisers. This was a period of exploration, and Zimmer was fascinated by how technology could be used to generate new and inventive sounds. He later noted how his work with The Buggles taught him how to manipulate and layer various parts, which would be useful in his film score career. Despite his success, Zimmer felt dissatisfied in the pop scene. He longed for a means to merge his love of music with storytelling on a larger scale, which led him to investigate the world of film.

Zimmer's journey into cinema scoring was not immediate or easy. It required a combination of chance contacts, a willingness to take chances, and a true enthusiasm for cinematic storytelling. One of the most major effects during this period was his meeting with composer Stanley Myers, who was already well-known in the film industry. Myers, best known for his work on films like The Deer Hunter (1978), became Zimmer's mentor, leading him through the nuances of film composition. Recognizing Zimmer's talent, Myers took him under his wing and together they established a tiny recording studio in London. This partnership served as a useful apprenticeship for Zimmer, teaching him the complexities of scoring and how music may enrich a film's narrative.

Under Myers' guidance, Zimmer began to establish his distinct style, which combined electronic elements with traditional orchestral arrangements. This combination was groundbreaking at the time, as most cinema scores used orchestral pieces. Zimmer's usage of synthesisers added a modern edge to his work, distinguishing him from his colleagues and identifying him as a composer capable of bringing something new to the business.

Zimmer's first major break in cinema scoring occurred in 1985, when he was selected to soundtrack My Beautiful Laundrette, a British comedy-drama directed by Stephen Frears. The film, set in London's South Asian community, featured the narrative of a young British-Pakistani man dealing with difficulties of identity, family, and societal expectations. Zimmer's score for My Beautiful Laundrette was innovative in its use of electronic music to convey the film's varied, multicultural setting. Zimmer's composition was both emotive and original, since it combined traditional South Asian musical patterns with contemporary synthesiser sounds. The music did more than just accompany the action; it enhanced the film's emotional depth and added levels of significance to the story.

Critics and spectators alike praised Zimmer's work on My Beautiful Laundrette for its uniqueness and ability to flawlessly integrate many musical styles. This project marked Zimmer's debut as a serious composer in the film industry, demonstrating his ability to cross genres by combining parts of classical, rock, and electronic music to create something completely unique.

Following the success of My Beautiful Laundrette, Zimmer continued to establish himself as a composer, and his next major opportunity came in 1988 with the film A World Apart, directed by Chris Menges. This film, set in apartheid-era South Africa, tells the narrative of a young girl growing up in the midst of political turbulence. It was a very emotional and hard film, and Zimmer was entrusted with composing a music that could reflect the story's complexity while being culturally and historically relevant.

For A World Apart, Zimmer exhibited his exceptional ability to combine many musical ideas to produce a score that was both eerie and hopeful. He mixed African rhythms and instruments with more traditional orchestral arrangements, creating a soundscape that evoked the film's setting while simultaneously emphasising the universal themes of love, grief, and survival. The score was acclaimed for its sensitivity and ability to heighten the film's emotional impact while not overpowering the story.

Zimmer's work on A World Apart helped him get more prominence in the film industry and reinforced his image as a composer who can handle difficult, emotionally charged films. It also constituted a watershed moment in his career, as it was the project that drew the attention of Hollywood. Around this time, Zimmer began to be recognized as an artist capable of elevating a film through his music, rather than just as a composer.

When discussing his shift from pop to film scoring, Zimmer frequently discusses the difficulties he encountered in adjusting to a new medium. In the pop world, he was accustomed to making music that stood on its own, music meant to be heard alone. However, cinema composing needed a different approach: he had to submit his music to the needs of the story, creating something that served rather than overpowered the film. This transition led him to reconsider his approach to composition, and it was through cooperation with filmmakers such as Stephen Frears and Chris Menges that Zimmer honed his technique.

Anecdotes from this time show Zimmer's unwavering work ethic and desire to experiment with fresh concepts. He would frequently spend long nights in the studio, experimenting with various sounds, combining synthesisers with traditional instruments, and investigating how different textures could elicit distinct feelings. This dedication and passion for music shone through in every film he worked on, and it wasn't long before his inventive approach drew the attention of Hollywood's most renowned directors and producers.

By the end of the 1980s, Hans Zimmer had established himself as one of the most promising young cinema composers. His work on My Beautiful Laundrette and A World Apart demonstrated his ability to combine various musical components to create compositions that were both emotionally moving and artistically distinct. These efforts were more than just career milestones; they demonstrated Zimmer's ability to reinvent film music.

The 1980s were a transformative decade for Hans Zimmer, as he moved from the synth-pop world of The Buggles to the cinematic vistas of film score. His journey was distinguished by a willingness to take risks, a commitment to his art, and a firm confidence in music's ability to tell stories. As he entered the next stage of his career, Zimmer took with him the lessons, influences, and experiences of this important decade, ready to continue on a path that would eventually lead him to become one of the most renowned cinema composers of his generation.

These early cinema scores provided the groundwork for what would become an extraordinary career, paving the way for the pioneering work that was to come. They were the initial steps in a journey that would take Hans Zimmer from London's studios to the heights of Hollywood, where he would continue to push the boundaries of what cinema music could accomplish.

CHAPTER 3

RISE TO PROMINENCE(1988–1995)

Between 1988 and 1995, Hans Zimmer's career in cinema scoring skyrocketed from budding talent to household celebrity. During this time, he progressed from a relatively obscure composer to one of Hollywood's most sought-after names. This meteoric rise was marked by his game-changing score for Rain Man, collaborations with renowned directors such as Ridley Scott, Tony Scott, and Barry Levinson, and the emergence of a signature sound that would define film music for years to come.

The Game-Changing Impact of Rain Man (1988)

Zimmer's breakthrough came when he composed the score for Barry Levinson's Rain Man (1988). The film, starring Dustin Hoffman and Tom Cruise, featured the moving story of a self-centered guy who discovers his estranged brother is an autistic savant. Levinson's decision to have Zimmer soundtrack the film proved to be a masterstroke. Instead of adhering to Hollywood orchestral standards, Zimmer created a soundtrack using synthesisers, marimbas, and strange rhythmic rhythms that seemed both current and highly evocative.

Zimmer's composition for Rain Man was more than just background music; it became an integral element of the tale, bringing emotional depth to critical moments. "Leaving Wallbrook," one of the most recognizable compositions, captures the film's narrative's mix of melancholy and hope. The repeating, simple music generated a haunting impact, conveying the two brothers' complicated emotions while without overshadowing the conversation or action. Zimmer stood out from other composers of his period due to his unique use of synthesisers and world music influences.

The Rain Man soundtrack's popularity was unquestionable. Zimmer received his first Academy Award nomination, and the film won four Oscars, including Best Picture. This accomplishment not only solidified Zimmer's name in Hollywood, but also established his ability to bring a new, modern perspective to film scoring. It was the impetus that pushed him to collaborate with some of the industry's biggest personalities.

Collaborations with Ridley Scott, Tony Scott, and Barry Levinson

Following Rain Man, Zimmer's career took off, and he began collaborating with high-profile directors, each of whom helped shape his changing style.

Ridley Scott films include Black Rain (1989), Thelma & Louise (1991), and 1492: Conquest of Paradise (1992).

One of Zimmer's most successful collaborations was with Ridley Scott, a director noted for his visually gorgeous and frequently epic films. Their first collaboration was Black Rain (1989), a criminal thriller set in Japan. Zimmer combined electronic components with traditional Japanese instruments to create an evocative sound that complemented the film's harsh urban backdrop. This blend of East and West, synthesisers and orchestral parts exemplified Zimmer's ability to tailor his music to the director's vision precisely.

Their subsequent collaboration, Thelma & Louise (1991), let Zimmer play with Americana influences. The score for the road movie caught the rebellious attitude and themes of emancipation, combining bluesy guitar riffs with beautiful synthesizer layers to give the picture a sense of adventure and sorrow. The music for Thelma & Louise was more than just a soundtrack; it served as a narrative element, helping to communicate the film's emotional depth.

Zimmer and Scott expanded their partnership with 1492: Conquest of Paradise (1992). This historical movie about Christopher Columbus' expedition needs a sweeping, grandiose soundtrack. Zimmer composed a soundtrack that combined orchestral compositions with choral elements, giving the film a sense of grandeur and revelation that fit its epic journey.

Tony Scott: Days of Thunder (1990), True Romance (1993).

Ridley Scott's brother, Tony Scott, was another filmmaker who frequently worked with Zimmer. The couple originally collaborated on the high-octane NASCAR picture Days of Thunder (1990), starring Tom Cruise. Zimmer's score for Days of Thunder evoked the energy and adrenaline of motor racing with throbbing rhythms and rock-influenced melodies. This method not only established the tone for the film, but also displayed Zimmer's ability to adapt his music to many genres.

Their next collaboration, True Romance (1993), demonstrated Zimmer's ability to combine many musical styles. For this Quentin Tarantino-directed picture, Zimmer composed a hauntingly beautiful score based on Carl Orff's "Gassenhauer." The marimba-driven theme gave the film a dreamy aspect that contrasted with its violent and chaotic plot. The juxtaposition of delicate, melodic melodies with the grim plot became one of the film's most memorable parts, demonstrating Zimmer's ability to use music to defy expectations.

Barry Levinson's Bugsy (1991)

Zimmer reunited with Barry Levinson for the 1991 biographical crime movie Bugsy, on the notorious criminal Bugsy Siegel. Zimmer opted for a more traditional orchestral approach for this picture, rather than using synths. He imbued the music with elegance and menace, evoking the splendor and volatility of 1940s Hollywood. The use of sweeping strings and jazz-inspired melodies demonstrated Zimmer's versatility and ability to adapt his music to diverse times and locations.

Notable Scores From Driving Miss Daisy to The Lion King

By the early 1990s, Zimmer had established a distinct style that combined orchestral parts with synthesisers and relied on a wide range of genres and cultural influences.

The score for Driving Miss Daisy (1989) was one of his most influential compositions at the time. The film, which follows the connection of an old Jewish widow and her African-American driver, required a soundtrack that was both sensitive and emotionally moving. Zimmer composed a soundtrack with piano, clarinet, and delicate synthesiser tones that nicely complimented the film's themes of friendship and change. The score was hailed for its simplicity and tenderness, and Zimmer received a Grammy Award nomination.

In Green Card (1990), Zimmer honed his ability to merge musical styles, integrating French-inspired accordion melodies with orchestral components to present a story about romance and cultural clash. Zimmer's versatility became a defining feature of his work, distinguishing him from other Hollywood composers.

His work on The Lion King (1994) marked a watershed moment in Zimmer's career. The animated film's score, which incorporated African rhythms, choral arrangements, and orchestral pieces, became one of the most memorable soundtracks of all time. Zimmer collaborated closely with South African artists, particularly Lebo M., to infuse realism into the score, adding unprecedented depth to the film's storytelling. The soundtrack's emotional breadth—from the triumphal "Circle of Life" to the heartbreaking "To

Die For"—showcased Zimmer's talent of creating music that could elicit a wide range of emotions.

Zimmer's score for The Lion King earned him his first Academy Award for Best Original Score, along with a Golden Globe and two Grammy Awards. This work not only cemented his position as a leading cinema composer, but also marked his debut as a global cultural figure.

Industry Recognition and Awards

Between 1988 and 1995, Zimmer received various awards and industry recognition. His soundtracks for Rain Man and The Lion King received Academy Award nominations, and his work with Ridley and Tony Scott, Barry Levinson, and other renowned directors cemented his reputation as one of Hollywood's most inventive composers. Zimmer's ability to combine numerous genres, instruments, and cultural influences set him apart in an industry that frequently favored traditional orchestral music.

Influence on Hollywood's Musical Landscape

By the mid-1990s, Hans Zimmer had not only gained recognition, but also drastically altered Hollywood's musical scene. His creative use of synthesisers, paired with his ability to incorporate worldwide musical influences into his work, established a new standard in cinema score. Zimmer's soundtracks were no longer just accompaniments; they were fundamental to the storytelling process, capable of heightening a film's emotional effect and generating an unforgettable cinematic experience.

Zimmer's ascent to prominence during this period was a reflection of his variety, innovation, and dedication to his profession. By combining electronic and orchestral components, working with a varied spectrum of directors, and pushing the bounds of traditional film scoring, Hans Zimmer reinvented what it meant to produce music for films. As he progressed beyond this era, Zimmer continued to innovate, laying the groundwork for even more remarkable work in the years ahead.

CHAPTER 4

CRAFTING ICONICS SCORING (1996–2005)

Between 1996 and 2005, Hans Zimmer experienced incredible growth, innovation, and impact. During this time, Zimmer redefined the action film soundtrack, established himself as a master of epic storytelling with his DreamWorks collaborations, and broadened his range to include multiple genres. This chapter digs into the unique techniques, noteworthy partnerships, and important compositions that shaped Zimmer's work during this pivotal decade.

Reinventing Action Scores: Crimson Tide (1995) and The Rock (1996)

Zimmer's innovation of action picture music began with Tony Scott's Crimson Tide (1995) and

culminated with Michael Bay's The Rock (1996).
Both films are considered milestones in action
music, with Zimmer's dramatic use of synthesisers,
orchestras, and thematic elements resulting in a
sound that became synonymous with 1990s action
cinema.

Crimson Tide: The Power of Orchestra

Crimson Tide demonstrated Zimmer's ability to
incorporate electronic elements into traditional
orchestral scoring. The main theme, which includes
forceful brass, martial percussion, and choral
harmonies, captures the intensity and drama of a
nuclear submarine standoff. Zimmer's theme gave
the film an incredible sense of intensity, making the
underwater clashes feel like epic battles. His use of
Gregorian chants, influenced by Russian liturgical
music, adds a melancholy element to the score,
resulting in a feeling of grandeur and peril.

Crimson Tide's soundtrack was pioneering, as it
was the first time a synthesiser score was regarded

with the same reverence as a classical orchestral piece. It was widely praised and established a model for action picture music, influencing other composers in the years that followed.

The Rock: Collaboration with Michael Bay

Zimmer's collaboration with Michael Bay on The Rock elevated his action score to a new level. The film's soundtrack, co-composed with Nick Glennie-Smith and Harry Gregson-Williams, featured driving rhythms, soaring trumpets, and rich, thematic melodies that added to the intensity of the action moments. The score's throbbing energy matched the film's high-octane thrills, and Zimmer's ability to merge electronic and orchestral components became the signature sound of Bay's blockbuster aesthetic.

The Rock's primary theme stands out for its unique melody, which captures the film's blend of courage and suspense. Zimmer's work on this picture cemented his reputation as a composer who can elevate action films with intricate, adrenaline-pumping compositions.

DreamWorks collaborations include The Prince of Egypt (1998) and Gladiator (2000).

Hans Zimmer's collaborations with DreamWorks helped shape his career and define the sound of epic storytelling. Zimmer collaborated with Jeffrey Katzenberg and Steven Spielberg to create some of modern cinema's most famous music.

The Prince of Egypt (1998): Creating a Biblical Epic.

The Prince of Egypt, an animated recreation of Moses' story, gave Zimmer the opportunity to explore themes of faith, redemption, and liberty via music. The score, which mixed traditional orchestral components with Middle Eastern instruments and choral arrangements, gave the film a sense of grandeur that suited its epic story. Zimmer worked with lyricist Stephen Schwartz to combine powerful melodies and emotive words, resulting in songs like "Deliver Us" and "When You Believe," which portrayed the film's emotional depth.

One of Zimmer's more inventive approaches in The Prince of Egypt was the incorporation of ethnic instruments like the duduk, a classic Armenian woodwind instrument. This lent authenticity and cultural depth to the score, bringing listeners to the ancient world. The soundtrack received widespread praise, earning several accolades and established Zimmer as a composer capable of mastering multiple genres and styles.

Gladiator (2000): Collaboration with Ridley Scott.

Zimmer's collaboration with director Ridley Scott in Gladiator was one of his most memorable moments. The picture, set in ancient Rome, needs a grandiose and emotionally powerful music. Zimmer partnered with singer Lisa Gerrard to create a melancholy, atmospheric music that has become one of the most well-known cinematic compositions in history.

The usage of voices, particularly on tunes like "Now We Are Free," gave the music a timeless feel, while Zimmer's blend of orchestral compositions and electronic components created a big and intimate ambiance. The score's "The Battle" theme became synonymous with epic cinema music, with Zimmer's trademark use of rhythmic strings, horns, and percussion to heighten suspense and excitement.

The Gladiator score won the Golden Globe for Best Original Score and was nominated for an Academy

Award, cementing Zimmer's status as an epic composer. Its influence stretched beyond the film itself, influencing the soundtracks of numerous historical dramas and action pictures that followed.

The Thin Red Line, The Last Samurai, and Pirates of the Caribbean

In the late 1990s and early 2000s, Zimmer broadened his repertoire by taking on projects that allowed him to experiment with other genres and push the boundaries of film score.

The Thin Red Line (1998): Collaboration with Terrence Malick

Working with filmmaker Terrence Malick on The Thin Red Line allowed Zimmer to create a score that was meditative, melancholy, and introspective. Unlike traditional war pictures, Malick's vision was poetic and philosophical, and Zimmer's music reflected this. The score is distinguished by its minimalist melodies, which frequently repeat simple themes to elicit emotional resonance.

One of the highlight tunes, "Journey to the Line," is a stunning composition that rises gradually, layering strings and brass to create a sense of impending disaster. This composition is one of Zimmer's most iconic pieces, and it has been frequently used in trailers and other media, demonstrating his ability to produce music that transcends the films for which it was initially written.

The Last Samurai (2003): Collaboration with Edward Zwick

Zimmer's composition for The Last Samurai was another foray into combining Western orchestral music and traditional Eastern elements. The film, set in nineteenth-century Japan, required music that captured both the grandeur of samurai society and the protagonist's emotional journey. Zimmer used Japanese instruments, like the taiko drum and shakuhachi flute, to create a realistic and immersive experience.

The score's sweeping motifs, notably in tunes like "A Way of Life" and "Safe Passage," demonstrated Zimmer's ability to convey a feeling of epic adventure while being emotionally grounded. The score for The Last Samurai was hailed for its beauty and complexity, adding to Zimmer's reputation for creating music that enhances the cinematic experience.

Pirates of the Caribbean: The Curse of the Black Pearl (2003): A New Type of Adventure Score

Zimmer's score for Pirates of the Caribbean: The Curse of the Black Pearl (2003) is among his most well-known. Although Klaus Badelt is technically acknowledged as the composer, Zimmer's influence can be seen throughout the music, as he worked as executive producer and contributed many of the important themes.

The soundtrack for Pirates of the Caribbean is distinguished by its lively, swashbuckling style, which combines orchestral parts with Zimmer's trademark usage of synthesisers and percussion.

The primary theme, "He's a Pirate," became an immediate classic, capturing the film's adventurous spirit and providing a sense of excitement to each action scene.

Zimmer's work on the Pirates of the Caribbean franchise transformed the sound of adventure films, prompting a new generation of composers to adopt a more dynamic, rhythmic approach to film score.

Industry Recognition and Awards

From 1996 until 2005, Hans Zimmer garnered numerous awards for his work, including Academy Award nominations, Golden Globes, and Grammy Awards. His soundtracks for The Prince of Egypt, Gladiator, and The Last Samurai received great acclaim, while his work on The Rock and Pirates of the Caribbean became famous in popular culture. Zimmer's ability to adapt his music to many genres and collaborate with some of Hollywood's most prominent directors cemented his reputation as one of the industry's leading composers.

Impact on Film Scoring and Popular Culture

Hans Zimmer's scores from 1996 to 2005 had a significant impact on the field of cinema scoring. His unique techniques, including combining electronic and orchestral components, ushered in a new era of grandiose and emotionally charged cinema music. Zimmer's work influenced other composers and helped to mold the sound of blockbuster films, establishing him as a defining voice in modern film music.

Zimmer's ability to generate memorable, evocative themes, paired with his eagerness to explore and push limits, ensured that his scores became an essential component of the films they accompanied. By the end of this decade, Hans Zimmer had solidified his reputation as a composer capable of creating legendary scores that not only enriched the films they accompanied, but also left an enduring impression on popular culture.

CHAPTER 5

AWARDS AND RECOGNITION

(1988–Present)

Hans Zimmer's illustrious career has spanned three decades, during which time he has revolutionised the landscape of film music, winning international praise and several awards. From winning his first Academy Award for The Lion King to his most recent triumph with Dune, Zimmer's career exemplifies his unrivalled brilliance and dedication. This chapter delves into his astounding accomplishments, focusing on the key accolades and honours that have cemented his reputation as one of the greatest cinema composers of all time.

Academy Awards and Nominations: From The Lion King to Dune

The Academy Awards, or Oscars, are the pinnacle of excellence in the film industry, and Hans Zimmer's involvement with these coveted awards began in 1989 with a nomination for Rain Man. His first major success occurred in 1995, when he won an Oscar for Best Original Score for The Lion King (1994).

The Lion King (1994): A Game-Changing Win.

Zimmer's score for The Lion King marked a watershed moment in his career, combining African rhythms, choral arrangements, and orchestral components to produce an epic and emotionally emotional soundtrack. The popularity of the film's soundtrack, which included legendary pieces such as "Circle of Life" and "Hakuna Matata," earned Zimmer his first Academy Award, establishing him as a powerhouse in cinema music. This accomplishment was not only a personal triumph, but also a watershed moment for the function of film music in animated narrative.

Subsequent Oscar nominations and wins.

Zimmer's Oscar odyssey continued, as he got nominations for additional outstanding scores, including:

Gladiator (2000) - Zimmer's cooperation with Ridley Scott on this epic historical drama won him another Academy Award nomination, and the music became one of his most recognizable.

Inception (2010) - Inception's dreamy, dramatic, and inventive soundscapes earned Zimmer another Oscar nomination, demonstrating his ability to combine electronic elements with classical orchestration.

Interstellar (2014) - Zimmer's collaboration with filmmaker Christopher Nolan reached new heights in Interstellar, winning him another nomination. The score's haunting organ melodies and ethereal tones reflected the film's themes of time, distance, and human emotion.

Zimmer earned his second Academy Award in 2022, for Dune (2021), over 30 years after his first. His groundbreaking score for Denis Villeneuve's adaptation of Frank Herbert's science fiction epic showcased Zimmer's ongoing development as a composer, incorporating experimental techniques, non-traditional instruments, and haunting choral work to create a soundscape that perfectly captured the film's otherworldly atmosphere.

Golden Globes, Grammys, and Other Notable Achievements

Zimmer's tremendous credentials go beyond the Oscars, with multiple Golden Globe and Grammy victories solidifying his place as one of the most acclaimed composers of our time.

Golden Globe Winners and Nominees

Zimmer has won three Golden Globes and gotten numerous nominations over his career:

The Lion King (1994) - Zimmer's first Golden Globe award coincided with his Oscar victory for The Lion King. The score's colourful and lyrical compositions captivated viewers around the world, making it one of the most memorable soundtracks in film history.

Gladiator (2000) - Zimmer won another Golden Globe for Gladiator, a composition that expertly mixed orchestral force and mournful vocals, with contributions from soprano Lisa Gerrard.

Dune (2021) - Zimmer's last Golden Globe triumph was for his inventive score for Dune, demonstrating that even after decades in the industry, he remains at the vanguard of cinematic music.

Zimmer has also received Golden Globe nominations for scores in Inception, The Thin Red Line (1998), and Interstellar, demonstrating his persistent excellence across multiple genres.

Grammy Awards and Recognition

Zimmer's influence on music extends to the Grammys, where he has received four awards:

Best Instrumental Arrangement with Accompanying Vocal(s) for The Lion King (1994) - Zimmer received a Grammy nomination for "Circle of Life," which he co-arranged.

Best Score Soundtrack for Visual Media for Crimson Tide (1995) - His creative action score was recognized, solidifying his name even more.

Zimmer has also received numerous nominations for his soundtracks, including Inception and The Dark Knight (2008), where he collaborated with James Newton Howard to introduce a darker, more powerful tone to superhero flicks.

BAFTA, Critics' Choice, and Other Awards

Aside from the Oscars, Golden Globes, and Grammys, Zimmer has garnered countless other major accolades, demonstrating his influence in the film business.

BAFTA Award: Zimmer received the British Academy of Film and Television Arts (BAFTA) Award for Best Film Music for Gladiator. This prize recognized the score's widespread appeal and importance in reinventing epic cinema music.

Critics' Choice Movie Awards: Zimmer has received numerous awards from the Critics' Choice Movie Awards, including a win for Dune in 2022, indicating his continuous relevance and originality in current cinema score.

Lifetime Achievement Awards: Recognizing Innovation

Zimmer's contributions to the field of film music have not gone unnoticed, as he has garnered numerous lifetime achievement awards that honour his long-term impact and inventiveness.

The American Society of Composers, Authors, and Publishers (ASCAP) Lifetime Achievement Award recognized Zimmer's outstanding career and influence on generations of composers. His ability to adapt cinema music has influenced other musicians, making him a respected figure in the business.

Max Steiner cinema Music Achievement honour: In 2018, Zimmer earned this honour at the annual Hollywood in Vienna event, which recognizes his remarkable contributions to cinema music. The prize, named for iconic composer Max Steiner, recognizes Zimmer as one of the greatest film composers of all time.

Zimmer received the World Soundtrack Lifetime Achievement Award in 2018, which recognized his exceptional body of work and role in converting film music into a crucial component of storytelling.

Honorary Doctorate and Degree

Zimmer's accomplishments have also been acknowledged by academic institutions. In 2019, he was awarded an Honorary Doctor of Music degree from the Royal College of Music in London, where he studied as a young musician. This distinction not only recognized his enormous contributions to music, but also represented a watershed moment in his progression from emerging artist to worldwide famous composer.

Influence on the Film Industry and Music Community

Hans Zimmer's influence goes far beyond his outstanding collection of prizes. His creative approach to cinema scoring has transformed the way music interacts with narrative storytelling. Zimmer's use of electronic components, non-traditional instrumentation, and the incorporation of cultural influences have established him as a pioneer in his area.

Zimmer's mentorship has influenced the next generation of composers. He has given developing artists such as John Powell, Harry Gregson-Williams, and Ramin Djawadi opportunities through his Remote Control Productions company, thereby contributing to the development of a new generation of cinema music composers.

From his revolutionary work on The Lion King to his recent win with Dune, Hans Zimmer's honours and recognition demonstrate his outstanding brilliance, innovation, and long-lasting impact on the world of film music. His path is more than just a collection of awards and honours; it reflects his enthusiasm for pushing the boundaries of musical storytelling. As Zimmer continues to write and inspire, his legacy is one of invention, quality, and steadfast dedication to the art of cinema music.

CHAPTER 6

EVOLUTION AND EXPERIMENTATION (2006–2015)

Between 2006 and 2015, Hans Zimmer's career skyrocketed, thanks to daring experimentation, inventive scoring approaches, and a slew of revolutionary collaborations, most notably with filmmaker Christopher Nolan. During this period, Zimmer not only rebuilt his personal style, but also transformed the landscape of film music, inspiring an entire generation of composers and pushing the film score to new heights.

The Nolan Era: The Dark Knight Trilogy, Inception

Zimmer's collaboration with Christopher Nolan was one of the most defining collaborations of his career, producing some of modern cinema's most memorable compositions.

Reimagining the Superhero Soundscape

The relationship began with Batman Begins (2005), but The Dark Knight (2008) solidified Zimmer's reputation as a cinematic music pioneer. Zimmer collaborated with composer James Newton Howard to create a gritty, dramatic, and entirely unique aural landscape that brilliantly captured the film's grim tone.

The Dark Knight (2008): The Development of a New Sound

Zimmer's approach to scoring The Dark Knight was innovative. He used unusual instruments, such as razor blades scraping piano wires, to produce the iconic, frightening two-note motif for the Joker, played by Heath Ledger. This motif was more than just a theme; it was a psychological portrayal of chaos and disorder. By eliminating melody and instead employing discordant and tension-building noises, Zimmer produced an aural portrayal of the Joker's unpredictable behaviour.

The score was critically acclaimed and earned numerous honours, including a Grammy for Best Score Soundtrack for Visual Media. Zimmer's work on The Dark Knight not only transformed superhero music, but also established new standards for how film scores might portray characters' psychological complexity.

Inception (2010): Into the World of Dreams

Zimmer and Nolan's partnership reached new heights with Inception (2010), which included Zimmer's music as a fundamental aspect of the film's narrative structure. The score, which featured massive brass, haunting string parts, and deep, resonating electronic pulses, contributed to the story's surreal, layered quality.

Zimmer's use of Édith Piaf's "Non, Je Ne Regrette Rien" was one of the most memorable elements of the Inception music. He slowed down the music to produce a disturbing, almost otherworldly effect that mirrored the concept of time dilation in the film's dream levels. This creative move demonstrated Zimmer's mastery of incorporating sound into the film's storyline, making the music an integral element of the storytelling experience.

The "BRAAAM" sound, a thunderous orchestral blast that has since become synonymous with trailers and action sequences, debuted with Inception. This breakthrough cemented Zimmer's status as a significant figure, as it changed how intensity and urgency might be conveyed through music. Zimmer's composition for Inception garnered him numerous honours and nominations, including an Academy Award nomination and a BAFTA win, cementing his reputation as one of the most innovative composers of his time.

Digital and Electronic Innovation: Interstellar and Beyond

During this time, Zimmer began experimenting with electronic elements, combining traditional orchestral arrangements with digital synthesisers to create soundtracks that were both emotionally strong and technologically sophisticated.

Interstellar (2014): A Cosmological Exploration

Zimmer's score for Interstellar (2014) is frequently regarded as one of his most ambitious and adventurous compositions. Nolan purposefully kept details of the film from Zimmer, offering only a brief letter describing a father-daughter connection, allowing Zimmer to write with emotional purity rather than focusing on the sci-fi elements. This produced a highly intimate and affecting composition.

One of Zimmer's most striking choices was to center the score on the organ, notably the 1926 Harrison & Harrison organ from London's Temple Church. This decision resulted in an ethereal, transcendent quality that complemented the film's themes of space exploration, time, and the human condition. The organ's deep, resonant tones evoked a sense of immensity, wonder, and isolation, capturing the endless aspect of space.

Zimmer used sounds like ticking clocks to play with tempo and repetition to reflect the concept of temporal relativity, particularly in moments when time distortion was an important narrative aspect. The score for Interstellar received widespread acclaim, giving Zimmer another Academy Award nomination and cementing his reputation for pushing the frontiers of cinema scoring.

Redefining Superhero Scores: Man of Steel and Batman vs Superman

Zimmer's work with director Zack Snyder on Man of Steel (2013) and Batman v Superman: Dawn of Justice (2016) heralded his return to the superhero genre, albeit from a completely different perspective.

Man of Steel (2013): Reinventing a Classic Hero

The task of writing the score for Man of Steel was daunting, given that John Williams' classic Superman theme from the 1978 picture was deeply embedded in popular culture. Zimmer, on the other hand, took a risk by creating a music that highlighted Superman's humanity and emotional depth.

Instead of traditional brass fanfare, Zimmer employed soaring strings, booming percussion, and an evocative 12-drummer ensemble to convey grandeur and valour. The use of many drummers represented Superman's great power and fury, while Zimmer's minimalist piano themes portrayed the character's vulnerability and psychological conflicts. The end result was an epic, emotive, and decidedly modern soundtrack that received acclaim for its originality and complexity.

Batman Vs. Superman: Dawn of Justice (2016): A Clash of Titans

For **Batman v Superman:** Dawn of Justice, Zimmer worked with Dutch composer Junkie XL (Tom Holkenborg) to produce a soundtrack that reflected the intensity of the film's themes. While Junkie XL handled the majority of the Batman music, Zimmer concentrated on developing and refining Superman's themes, mixing orchestral parts with electronic sounds to underline the conflict between the two legendary heroes.

The film's score demonstrated Zimmer's ability to adapt and evolve by combining traditional orchestration with cutting-edge technology.

Although Zimmer announced his departure from superhero films following this production, his impact on the genre is unmistakable, with many future superhero soundtracks deriving inspiration from his work.

Innovative Scoring Techniques and Industry Impact

Zimmer's work from 2006 to 2015 is distinguished by his willingness to explore new territory and deviate from traditional scoring approaches. His use of unusual instruments, technological experimentation, and the incorporation of music into the narrative structure of films impacted many composers, creating the sound of modern cinema.

One of Zimmer's most inventive methods during this period was the use of minimalism, as seen in Interstellar and Inception. By reducing melodies to their fundamental elements, Zimmer created soundtracks that were more about emotion and mood than sophisticated orchestration. This method enabled the music to serve as an extension of the story rather than simply accompanying it.

Critical Reception and Awards

Zimmer's scores during this period were widely acclaimed, earning him multiple prizes and nominations.

Zimmer received an Academy Award nomination for Interstellar (2014).

Grammy Awards: Zimmer won Best Score Soundtrack for Visual Media for The Dark Knight (2008) and was nominated for Inception and Interstellar.

Zimmer won the Golden Globe for Inception (2010) and was nominated for Interstellar.

These awards not only celebrate Zimmer's individual accomplishments, but also his overall impact on the cinema industry. His ability to combine traditional orchestral arrangements with electronic and digital components has broadened the scope of what film music can accomplish, influencing composers across genres and media.

A Decade of Transformation

From 2006 to 2015, Hans Zimmer's development and experimentation were among his most noteworthy achievements. Zimmer has established himself as a film music visionary through collaborations with Christopher Nolan, pioneering use of digital and electronic components, and redefining superhero compositions. His ability to push limits, embrace new technology, and challenge traditional expectations has not only enhanced the films on which he has worked, but has also left an indelible mark on the art of film scoring. This time exemplifies Zimmer's creative talent and lasting impact on the world of cinema.

CHAPTER 7

COLLABORATIVE GENIUS —
PARTNERSHIP AND INFLUENCE

Hans Zimmer's career demonstrates the power of collaboration. Over the years, he has distinguished himself not just as an outstanding composer, but also as a collaborative genius who lives on creative collaborations. This chapter explores Zimmer's dynamic relationships with creative directors, fellow composers, and the next generation of artists, illuminating how these partnerships influenced his legendary soundtracks while also leaving an enduring mark on the cinema and music industries.

Director Partnerships: Creating Cinematic Masterpieces

Hans Zimmer's career is defined by his profound, long-standing ties with some of the film industry's most recognized filmmakers. His collaborations with Ridley Scott, Christopher Nolan, and Denis Villeneuve demonstrate how a shared vision may result in unique cinematic experiences.

Ridley Scott: Creating Epic Worlds

Zimmer's partnership with Ridley Scott began with Thelma and Louise (1991), but it reached new heights with Gladiator (2000). Gladiator's score is one of Zimmer's most acclaimed works, and it is widely regarded as a watershed moment in his professional career. During this production, Zimmer and vocalist Lisa Gerrard created a soundtrack that combined orchestral elements with ancient, haunting vocals, resulting in a timeless and emotional backdrop for Scott's epic tale of revenge and redemption.

Zimmer and Scott's collaboration is distinguished by a shared understanding of storytelling through music. Scott previously praised Zimmer's ability to "paint pictures with sound," which is obvious in how Zimmer's music enhances the visual experience of Scott's films. Their partnership continued with films like Hannibal (2001) and Black Hawk Down (2001), with each piece demonstrating Zimmer's adaptability to Scott's many storytelling methods.

The Gladiator score earned a Golden Globe and was nominated for an Academy Award, illustrating how Zimmer's collaboration with Scott contributed significantly to the film's emotional depth and popularity. This cooperation established the tone for Zimmer's subsequent productions, demonstrating that when a composer and director have a shared vision, the results may be really revolutionary.

Christopher Nolan is shaping modern film music

Perhaps the most memorable of Zimmer's director partnerships is his work with Christopher Nolan, which began with Batman Begins (2005) and lasted a decade, delivering some of the most influential film scores of the twenty-first century. Zimmer's work on The Dark Knight Trilogy, Inception (2010), and Interstellar (2014) revolutionised the way music might be used to improve cinematic storytelling.

Nolan's approach to filmmaking is sophisticated and multidimensional, and he frequently pushes Zimmer to go outside of his comfort zone. For The Dark Knight (2008), Nolan asked Zimmer to develop a disturbing and austere tune for the Joker, resulting in the now-famous two-note motif that brilliantly represented the character's turmoil and unpredictability. Zimmer has credited Nolan with encouraging him to experiment with new sounds and approaches, which resulted in unique scoring methods such as utilising razor blades on piano strings or merging orchestral arrangements with electronic components.

Their partnership on Inception elevated Zimmer's inventiveness to unprecedented heights. The inclusion of Édith Piaf's "Non, Je Ne Regrette Rien," slowed down and integrated into the score, became a vital aspect of the film's plot, showcasing the breadth of their creative collaboration. Zimmer has frequently discussed how Nolan's willingness to experiment and embrace the unexpected enabled him to deviate from typical score frameworks, resulting in a soundtrack that was as much a character in the film as the performers.

Zimmer's collaboration with Nolan culminated in Interstellar, where Zimmer's use of the organ created a vast, otherworldly soundtrack. Nolan's insistence on focusing on the emotional core of the story, rather than the science-fiction components, allowed Zimmer to create an intimate yet grandiose music, confirming their reputation as one of modern cinema's most successful director-composer duos.

Denis Villeneuve, A New Frontier

Zimmer's more recent cooperation with Denis Villeneuve on Dune (2021) demonstrated his willingness to explore unexplored regions. Villeneuve, a creative director recognized for his attention to detail and atmospheric narrative, tasked Zimmer with creating a score that felt completely alien and unlike anything heard before.

Zimmer's approach to Dune was abandoning traditional orchestration in favour of fresh, experimental sounds that complemented the film's extraterrestrial environment. He used instruments from diverse civilizations, strange vocal styles, and even custom-made instruments to create the distinctive environment Villeneuve envisioned. Zimmer's partnership with Villeneuve demonstrated his commitment to pushing the boundaries and reinventing what film music can be.

Composer Collaborations: Combining Styles and Innovating

In addition to working with filmmakers, Zimmer has frequently collaborated with other composers, producing some of his most original and memorable soundtracks. These collaborations show Zimmer's generosity as an artist, openness to learn from others, and ability to blend various musical styles into a unified sound.

James Newton Howard's Dark Knight Trilogy

Zimmer's cooperation with James Newton Howard on Batman Begins and The Dark Knight exemplifies how two composers with different styles can work together to achieve something spectacular. While Zimmer concentrated on raw fury and enormous themes, Howard added a more melodic, emotional element, notably in moments depicting Bruce Wayne's personal difficulties.

Despite their disparate styles, the two composers collaborated seamlessly. Howard reportedly described their relationship as "like a dance," with each supporting the other's abilities. Their collaboration on The Dark Knight resulted in a soundtrack that was not only innovative, but also set the standard for superhero music in modern film.

Junkie XL (Tom Holkenborg): The Beginnings of a New Sound

Zimmer's relationship with Junkie XL, aka Tom Holkenborg, began with Man of Steel (2013) and continued with Batman v Superman: Dawn of Justice (2016). Junkie XL added a new, electronic edge to Zimmer's symphonic roots, yielding soundtracks that were both strong and current.

One of their most prominent collaborations was on Mad Max: Fury Road (2015), in which Junkie XL served as the principal composer while Zimmer provided substantial inspiration and guidance. The score's relentless energy and industrial sound complemented the film's post-apocalyptic style, demonstrating how Zimmer's influence shaped the project's auditory experience.

Lisa Gerrard: A fusion of voices and emotions

Zimmer's collaboration with Lisa Gerrard on Gladiator is still one of the most renowned collaborations in film music history. Gerrard's ghostly voice gave a haunting, emotional depth to the score, transforming it from a standard orchestral soundtrack into an otherworldly experience.

Zimmer has frequently mentioned how Gerrard's efforts added a feeling of sincerity and heart to the music, changing it into something that resonated strongly with audiences. This collaboration not only earned a Golden Globe, but also showcased Zimmer's willingness to combine his approach with performers from many genres, culminating in a timeless classic.

Mentoring the Next Generation: Hans Zimmer's Enduring Influence

Aside from his own work, Hans Zimmer has played an important role in mentoring and influencing the next generation of composers. He started Remote Control Productions, a music studio that has served as a training ground for new talent, cultivating a community of composers who have gone on to make substantial contributions to the film business.

Zimmer has trained composers including Lorne Balfe (Mission: Impossible - Fallout), Steve Mazzaro (The Boss Baby), and Ramin Djawadi (Game of Thrones). Zimmer's eagerness to share his expertise, skills, and industry insights has helped shape these composers' careers, ensuring that his impact goes far beyond his own productions.

Zimmer frequently discusses the value of teamwork and mentorship, emphasising that film score is not a solo undertaking. He believes that sharing ideas and collaborating with others strengthens the creative process, and this mindset has become a pillar of his legacy.

Impact on Film Scoring and the Music Industry.

Zimmer's collaborative spirit transformed the film scoring industry. Zimmer has broadened the possibilities of film music by breaking down genre barriers, embracing digital and electronic elements, and cultivating a mentorship culture.

His influence can be seen in how modern film scores have evolved, with many composers following his ideas, such as combining electronic and orchestral parts, using unorthodox instruments, and incorporating sound design into storytelling.

Hans Zimmer's career as a creative genius exemplifies the power of collaboration, mentoring, and creativity. His collaborations with directors such as Ridley Scott, Christopher Nolan, and Denis Villeneuve have produced some of the most memorable compositions in cinematic history. Meanwhile, his collaborations with other composers and mentoring of the next generation have ensured that his influence will be felt for many years to come.

Zimmer's legacy is defined not only by the music he has created, but also by the spirit of collaboration, innovation, and discovery that he represents. This chapter serves as a reminder that, while Zimmer is unquestionably a master of his trade, it is his openness to embrace others' ideas, abilities, and visions that distinguishes him as a film score legend.

CHAPTER 8

RECENT WORKS AND LEGACY

(2016–Present)

Hans Zimmer's career has not only spanned decades, but it has also changed to reflect the shifting world of film and music. Zimmer continued to develop his profession in the late 2010s and beyond, working with a new generation of filmmakers and experimenting with new musical techniques. This chapter delves into Zimmer's most recent compositions, from 2016 to the present, emphasising his broadening horizons, rethinking of classics, and lasting legacy in the film score industry.

Expanding Horizons: Notable Scores from 2016–Present

In the years since 2016, Hans Zimmer has continued to push the boundaries of his talent, creating astonishing compositions that have received critical praise and financial success.

Dunkirk (2017)

Christopher Nolan's Dunkirk constituted a watershed moment in Zimmer's career, demonstrating his ability to combine creative sound design with traditional score techniques. The film, which depicts the traumatic evacuation of Allied forces from Dunkirk during WWII, is noted for its non-linear storyline and minimalist sound design.

Zimmer's score uses a unique ticking clock motif to represent the unrelenting passage of time, reflecting the film's narrative and producing real tension. This motif is interlaced with a disturbing orchestral arrangement, creating a soundscape that keeps audiences on the edge of their seats. In an interview, Zimmer described the soundtrack as "an emotional heartbeat," representing the urgency and desperation of the protagonists' situation. The unique use of sound design, such as the integration of ambient noises and the modulation of instrumental textures, increased the film's impact, making it one of Zimmer's most praised works to date.

Dunkirk garnered numerous award nominations, including an Academy Award for Best Original Score, cementing Zimmer's status as a master of modern film composition.

Wonder Woman (2017)

While Zimmer's role in Wonder Woman was mostly as a collaborator, his impact may be seen in the film's memorable motifs. Zimmer collaborated with composer Rupert Gregson-Williams to create thematic material that became identified with the persona Diana Prince. The bold, soaring motifs conveyed a sense of strength and courage, which resonated with spectators and contributed to the movie's popularity.

Zimmer's themes were later used and expanded upon in the sequel, Wonder Woman 1984 (2020), demonstrating his ability to build memorable musical identities that transcend particular films. In a behind-the-scenes interview, Zimmer indicated a desire to contribute to female-led storylines in Hollywood, implying a personal involvement in the project that went beyond composing.

No Time to Die (2021)

Hans Zimmer's work on No Time to Die marks his first appearance in the renowned James Bond franchise, a long-awaited milestone for the composer. Working with director Cary Joji Fukunaga, Zimmer was charged with combining tradition and creativity, creating a music that honors the series' past while incorporating modern elements.

The score's combination of orchestral orchestration and current electronic sounds represents the Bond franchise's developing nature. Zimmer used motifs from past Bond soundtracks while also incorporating new themes to capture the emotional depth of Daniel Craig's interpretation of the role. His work with Billie Eilish, who performed the film's title song, provided a new layer of intricacy to the soundtrack, fusing the traditional and modern in a way that has become synonymous with current film music.

Reimagining Classics: Dune (2021)

One of Zimmer's most notable recent works is his soundtrack for Denis Villeneuve's Dune, a remake of Frank Herbert's famous science fiction novel. Zimmer's approach to Dune was groundbreaking; he intended to create a soundscape that transported spectators to the desert world of Arrakis by incorporating unusual instruments and vocal approaches.

The mix of chanting, throat singing, and odd percussive sounds provides an immersive environment that reflects the film's broad visual scene. Zimmer's commitment to authenticity includes collaborating with artists from diverse cultures to ensure that the score authentically reflected the film's themes and setting.

In an interview with Rolling Stone, Zimmer noted that he intended the soundtrack to feel like a "character" in and of itself, adding to the film's narrative and emotional impact. The score's rich textures and inventive ideas have earned critical praise, with many hailing it as one of Zimmer's best works.

Dune not only displayed Zimmer's maturing technique, but it also had an impact on the sci-fi genre, setting a new bar for modern film soundtracks. Its triumph at awards shows, including the Academy Award for Best Original Score, solidified Zimmer's reputation as a key player in film music.

Current projects and future endeavours

As of 2024, Hans Zimmer is still as productive and imaginative as ever, with numerous future projects that promise to highlight his continuous development as a composer. Notable prospective collaborations include working on Dune: Part Two (2024) with Villeneuve, where he hopes to elaborate on the subject material provided in the previous film.

Zimmer is also due to collaborate with director Guillermo del Toro on an unannounced project, which has piqued the interest of both fans and reviewers. Del Toro is known for his innovative storyline and distinct visual style, and his collaboration with Zimmer is expected to produce a score that flawlessly merges imagination and emotion.

Zimmer's continued commitment to mentoring aspiring composers through his Remote Control Productions company guarantees that his impact extends beyond his own works. His drive to developing new talent demonstrates his knowledge of the value of collaboration in the creative process.

Industry Recognition and Awards

Zimmer has received numerous awards in recent years for his contributions to film music. In addition to his Academy Awards, Zimmer has had other nominations and wins from major organisations such as the Golden Globes, BAFTA Awards, and Grammy Awards.

His work for Dune received widespread recognition, with critics praising the score's original nature and emotional depth. In 2022, Zimmer received the renowned Hans Christian Andersen Award for his contributions to music, emphasising his influence on the industry and ability to inspire future generations.

Establishing Hans Zimmer's Status as a Film Scoring Icon.

Hans Zimmer's most recent works show a career marked by both innovation and tradition. His ability to adapt to new techniques, accept collaboration, and push the frontiers of film score cements his place as a modern cinematic great.

Zimmer's influence goes beyond his individual scores; he has transformed the film music environment, inspiring a new generation of composers to explore with sound and storytelling. His collaborations with directors and fellow musicians have resulted in some of the most iconic film scores in history, and his mentorship initiatives will ensure that his legacy lives on for years to come..

As we consider Hans Zimmer's latest works and ongoing legacy, it becomes clear that his career as a composer is far from ended. His ongoing investigation of sound, combined with his dedication to collaboration and teaching, ensures that he will remain a key player in the cinema business for the foreseeable future.

With each endeavour, Zimmer invites viewers to explore the emotional depth and complexity of storytelling through music. Hans Zimmer's career as a composer reminds us of the unlimited possibilities of film scoring and the lasting impact of music on our shared cinematic experiences.

CHAPTER 9

PERSONAL LIFE AND PHILOSOPHY

Hans Zimmer, a name synonymous with cinematic music, has left a lasting legacy in the film business and beyond. While his scores elicit a wide range of emotions, the guy behind the music is equally captivating. This chapter delves into Zimmer's personal life and philosophy, highlighting the relationships, influences, and values that shape his work.

Family, Friendship, and Inspiration

Hans Zimmer was born on September 12, 1957, in Frankfurt, Germany, to a non-musical household. His father was an engineer, and his mother worked in a retail store, yet it was in this seemingly everyday environment that Zimmer's love of music blossomed. In several interviews, he has described how he found refuge in music as a child, frequently playing with sounds on the family piano. This early passion paved the way for his future career, however it took him some time to completely embrace his calling.

Family Influence

Zimmer's background instilled in him the qualities of tenacity and creativity. His mother, in particular, played an important role in encouraging him to follow his hobbies. In a heartfelt comment, Zimmer wrote, "My mother always told me that music is a way to communicate when words fail." This attitude has served as a guiding principle throughout his career, influencing how he views film score as a storytelling medium.

Despite his professional achievement, Zimmer remains close to his family. His relationships with his children affected his outlook on life and work. In interviews, he has emphasised the need of balancing his hard work with being a responsible father. This commitment to family reflects his conviction in cultivating creativity in a supportive atmosphere, which he also applies to his mentorship of budding composers.

Friendship and Collaboration

Throughout his career, Zimmer has developed strong friendships that go beyond business collaborations. One of his most renowned collaborations is with filmmaker Christopher Nolan, with whom he has composed some of the most memorable film scores in recent memory, including Inception and Dunkirk. Their shared vision for narrative reflects their creative synergy. Zimmer once said, "Working with Chris is like breathing; we just understand each other."

Zimmer's friendships extend to other composers as well. His collaborations with James Newton Howard on The Dark Knight and Lisa Gerrard on Gladiator demonstrate the strength of artistic friendship. He believes that collaboration fosters creativity, saying, "The best music often comes from a space where egos are left at the door."

Artistic Vision and the Creative Process

Zimmer's worldview is based on a belief in art's transforming power. He sees music as a link between emotions and stories, frequently declaring, "Music is the emotional language of cinema." This viewpoint directs his creative process, allowing him to explore the psychological qualities of characters and plots.

Zimmer's creative process is just as dynamic as the music he makes. He frequently starts with a conceptual framework, enabling ideas to develop organically. This agility is essential in a sector where the terrain is continuously changing. He embraces technology and uses digital tools to explore soundscapes and textures. In a discussion regarding the future of film score, Zimmer voiced his enthusiasm for technical improvements, saying, "The tools we have now are limitless." "It is an exciting time to be a composer."

Philosophy of Film Scoring's Role in Storytelling

For Zimmer, film score is an essential component of storytelling. He believes that music has the ability to elicit emotions, enrich tales, and foster a stronger bond between the audience and the characters on film. In his words, "A film score should make you feel like you're inside the story, not just watching it." This philosophy motivates him to produce soundtracks that connect with viewers on a personal level, inviting them into the film's emotional core.

His scores frequently demonstrate a great awareness of the human experience, combining orchestral arrangements with contemporary themes. This ability to cross genres has cemented Zimmer's reputation as a leader in the film scoring industry, motivating a new generation of composers to push the frontiers of musical storytelling.

Overcoming Challenges and Maintaining Passion

Despite his enormous success, Zimmer has experienced numerous hurdles, including self-doubt and criticism. He has openly discussed his battles with anxiousness, particularly in the early phases of his career. "There were times when I felt like I wasn't good enough," he said in an interview. However, Zimmer's resilience and love of music spurred him ahead, allowing him to embrace his distinct style and voice.

To keep his passion alive, Zimmer prioritises creative inquiry. He frequently takes on projects outside of his comfort zone, looking for opportunities to explore other techniques and genres. "Every score is a new adventure," he says, underlining the significance of keeping the creative process interesting and novel.

philanthropic endeavours and charitable work

Aside from his musical accomplishments, Zimmer is dedicated to philanthropy. He supports a number of humanitarian organisations, including the Music for Life Foundation, which works to give music instruction to neglected populations. Zimmer recognizes the enormous importance of music on personal development and creativity, noting, "Music is a gift, and everyone should have the opportunity to enjoy it."

His commitment to giving back demonstrates his conviction in the transforming potential of art. Zimmer hopes that by offering opportunities for young musicians, he may inspire the next generation to follow their dreams and express themselves through music.

Hope for Future Generations

As Zimmer contemplates his career, he evaluates his legacy not only in terms of the scores he has written, but also in terms of the influence he has had on others. He wishes to inspire aspiring songwriters to value their uniqueness and originality. "The future of film scoring is bright," the composer says. "We're entering an era where innovation is key, and I want to encourage young artists to take risks and find their own voices."

Zimmer's commitment to talent development extends beyond his own job. His mentorship of budding composers, as well as his involvement in educational activities, demonstrate his belief in the value of information sharing and creativity in the community.

Hans Zimmer's personal life and ideas depict a complex personality whose experiences have influenced his creativity. Through his family, connections, and creative partnerships, he exemplifies a collaborative spirit and a passion for music that is deeply felt in the business.

His perspectives on art and storytelling highlight the critical role film soundtrack plays in crafting cinematic experiences. Zimmer's ability to overcome obstacles while maintaining his enthusiasm for music demonstrates his perseverance and dedication to his work.

As he continues to influence the next generation of composers, Zimmer's status as a film scoring icon is solidified. His heartfelt dedication to philanthropy and mentorship guarantees that music's transforming power continues to thrive, affecting the lives of audiences and aspiring artists for many years to come. In Zimmer's words, "Music is a journey, and I'm excited to see where it takes us next."

CHAPTER 10

LEGACY AND CULTURAL IMPACTS

Hans Zimmer's impact on film scoring and music extends beyond the cinematic sphere, making him an important figure in current society. This chapter goes into Zimmer's enormous legacy, exploring the "Zimmer Effect" in popular culture, his contributions to live performances, and his transition from film to stage productions. We will look at how Zimmer's work continues to alter the musical environment and resonate with audiences all across the world, using expert views, anecdotes, and examples.

Impact on Pop Culture and Mainstream Music

The "Zimmer Effect" describes Hans Zimmer's ubiquitous effect on modern film scoring and beyond. His novel technique of combining orchestral music with electronic elements has established a new benchmark for film composers. Zimmer's soundtracks are notable for their emotional depth, thematic complexity, and creative soundscapes. Notably, the score for Inception (2010) charmed audiences and penetrated popular music. The characteristic "braaam" sound—a deep, resonant note that became a trademark of the film—has been frequently referenced and imitated in a variety of media, including trailers and memes.

Zimmer's ability to produce memorable themes has had a long-lasting impact on popular culture. His soundtracks for blockbuster films including The Dark Knight Trilogy, Gladiator, and Pirates of the Caribbean have entered the public awareness. In fact, tracks from these scores are frequently used in advertisements, athletic events, and even political rallies, demonstrating Zimmer's ability to elicit strong emotions and connect with audiences outside of the film world. Dr. Karen Collins, a musicologist, adds that "Zimmer's compositions have become cultural touchstones, defining the sound of modern cinema."

Zimmer's impact extends to modern musicians across genres. Musicians such as Hanz Zimmer (not to be confused with the composer) and electronic musicians such as ODESZA credit Zimmer as a major influence on their sound. The combination of orchestral parts with electronic music in popular songs reflects Zimmer's pioneering thematic depth, causing a ripple effect that encourages aspiring composers and producers around the world.

Contributions to concerts and live performances

Zimmer's influence extends beyond movies; his live performances have changed the concert experience as well. The Hans Zimmer Live concert series, which features his legendary works performed with full orchestras, has received international praise. These concerts provide an immersive experience for fans by merging live music with breathtaking visual aspects from the films, resulting in a dynamic and engaging ambiance.

One of the highlights of Zimmer's concert series is the Inception Live event, in which the film is shown as Zimmer conducts a live orchestra that plays the soundtrack. This unique combination of cinema and music allows listeners to experience the emotional intensity of his songs in real time. Audience members' testimonials usually emphasise the intense feelings evoked by these performances. "It was like being inside the movie," said one concertgoer, evoking how Zimmer's music transforms the cinematic experience into a live, shared encounter.

Zimmer has also worked with a variety of artists and orchestras, broadening the scope of his live shows. His collaborations with prominent performers, such as cellist Yo-Yo Ma and rock band The Who, demonstrate his adaptability and willingness to experiment across genres. According to music reviewer Tim Broughton, "Zimmer's ability to adapt his compositions for different settings showcases his understanding of music as a collaborative art form."

From Film to Stage: Expanding Horizons

Zimmer has recently broadened his horizons by experimenting with musical theatre and stage plays. His work on The Lion King (1994) is still one of his most recognized achievements, garnering him an Academy Award and a Grammy. The musical adaption of The Lion King, which debuted on Broadway, includes Zimmer's original composition and has become a global sensation in its own right.

In addition to The Lion King, Zimmer has worked on other stage projects, including the Gladiator live concert, which combines film and live performance in a theatrical environment. These pieces show Zimmer's dedication to exploring new artistic directions while retaining his characteristic sound.

Zimmer's recent cooperation with filmmaker Denis Villeneuve on the Dune (2021) score is another watershed moment in his career. This soundtrack not only pays homage to Frank Herbert's literary masterwork, but it also demonstrates Zimmer's capacity to innovate in the science fiction genre. The usage of unorthodox instruments and voice elements indicates his constant desire to push the frontiers of music composition. In an interview, Villeneuve stated, "Hans has a unique ability to create a sound world that is both familiar and alien, perfectly capturing the essence of Dune."

Philanthropic and educational initiatives

Zimmer's impact goes beyond his musical accomplishments; he is also committed to philanthropy and education. He actively supports projects to encourage music education, particularly in marginalized communities. Zimmer has collaborated with groups such as Music for Life to create opportunities for young musicians to improve their talents and pursue their passions.

In interviews, Zimmer frequently highlights the need of developing potential in the next generation. He believes that access to music education may change people's lives and stimulate creativity. "Music is a universal language," he says, "and it has the power to connect people across cultures and backgrounds." His philanthropic activities reflect his desire to ensure that everyone has access to music's transformational power.

Numerous industry professionals have acknowledged Zimmer's effect. Dr. Susan McClary, a musicologist, writes, "Zimmer's scores have redefined the expectations of film music, elevating it to a central role in storytelling." She emphasises the emotional complexity inherent in Zimmer's works, which frequently mimic the nuances of human experience.

Critics have highlighted that Zimmer's work symbolises a transition in how film music is regarded, from background support to a critical component of cinematic storylines. His ability to create ideas that appeal to listeners has set a new benchmark for modern composers. Film writer Richard Roeper writes that "Zimmer's scores are not just music; they are characters in their own right, adding layers to the films they accompany."

Audience insights and anecdotes

Fans of Zimmer frequently relate personal experiences on how his music has changed their lives. Zimmer's soundtracks have served as the music to numerous momentous events, including weddings and graduations. One admirer wrote, "The Gladiator music was played at my father's memorial ceremony. It captured his essence and provided comfort to our family during a terrible moment." Such testimonials demonstrate viewers' strong emotional connection to Zimmer's music.

Behind-the-scenes stories highlight the collaborative aspect of his work. Zimmer is noted for cultivating a creative environment in his studio, frequently asking young composers to offer ideas. "He's like a musical mentor," said composer Lorne Balfe, who has collaborated closely with Zimmer. "He encourages experimentation and values every voice in the room."

CONCLUSION

Hans Zimmer's impact is indelible in the cultural environment, defined by his innovative contributions to cinema scoring, live performances, and stage shows. The "Zimmer Effect" has changed current music expectations, impacting a diverse range of performers and genres. His ability to connect with fans on an emotional level ensures that his music transcends generations.

As Zimmer broadens his views and mentors the next generation of composers, his influence will definitely survive. He ensures that everyone has access to music's transforming potential through his humanitarian endeavours and commitment to music education. In the broad tapestry of cultural icons, Hans Zimmer stands out as a light of originality and invention, having made an unmistakable impression on the worlds of music and movies.

As the curtain falls on this trip through Hans Zimmer's extraordinary life and career, we are left with a lasting impression of a visionary composer who has transformed the landscape of film music. Zimmer's influence spans decades, and his imprint on popular culture is obvious. His classic tunes have become ingrained in our collective consciousness, eliciting emotions and transporting us to worlds both familiar and unfamiliar.

Zimmer's unwavering pursuit of innovation and artistic greatness has inspired generations of musicians, composers, and filmmakers. His impact stretches far beyond the silver screen, echoing in concert halls, arenas, and living rooms throughout the world. As a master of his trade, he has advanced film scoring by pushing limits and increasing the possibilities of musical storytelling.

Zimmer's extraordinary journey demonstrates the power of passion, dedication, and collaboration. From his humble beginnings in post-war Germany to his current standing as a Hollywood celebrity, his biography is a source of hope and inspiration. His legacy reminds us of music's transforming power to unite, heal, and transcend.

As we consider Hans Zimmer's incredible life and career, we are reminded of the timeless value of art in our lives. His music continues to enchant audiences, inspiring imagination and innovation. As we look ahead, we can be confident that Zimmer's legacy will survive, inspiring new generations of artists, composers, and visionaries.

According to Hans Zimmer, "Music is the only language that can touch your heart, mind, and soul simultaneously." His amazing history exemplifies this fundamental fact, leaving an unforgettable impression on the worlds of music, film, and beyond.

As the biography's final notes fade, Hans Zimmer's legendary themes reverberate in our thoughts and hearts, reminding us of music's transforming power to touch, inspire, and unite.

Thanks for Reading

Made in United States
Troutdale, OR
12/04/2024

25668869R00066